Glenna

all best wishes

Betty Wright

Overleaf: HORNBY AND BARLOW *See page 29*

A.N. HORNBY AND DICK BARLOW

CRICKET'S GOLDEN SUMMER

·PAINTINGS·IN·A·GARDEN·
·BY·GERRY·WRIGHT·
·WITH·A·COMMENTARY·
·BY·DAVID·FRITH·

PAVILION
MICHAEL JOSEPH

First published in Great Britain in 1985 by
Pavilion Books Limited
196 Shaftesbury Avenue, London WC2H 8JL
in association with Michael Joseph Limited
44 Bedford Square, London WC1B 3DU

ISBN 0 907516 67 X

The publishers would like to express their thanks
to Charles Fry, Malcolm Hamer, Keith Ireland, John Manley,
Roger Mann, Michael Parkinson, Rob Shreeve and Lord Weymouth,
for giving permission for the paintings in their
possession to be photographed.

Photographs by Peter Dazeley

Designed by Lawrence Edwards

Filmset in Great Britain by Butler & Tanner Ltd
Colour reproduction by Minervascan Ltd
Printed and bound in Italy by Arnoldo Mondadori

CONTENTS

The Village Team

Preface

N THE ABRASIVE age in which we live, where violence and cynicism, atheism and anarchy are such recurring themes as almost to be keystones of everyday life, it is excusable to seek momentary comfort in being wafted away to another age, when manners were gentle, man ruled machine, income tax was 8d (3p) in the £, and a glow of seemingly eternal summer warmed the land.

Not even the most careworn supplicant should subscribe unquestioningly to such an extreme view, of course, for violence there has always been, while medical advances have accelerated to our emphatic advantage, and the path to affluence is wider and better lit.

In terms of mental equilibrium, though, man would seem to be facing greater hazards today. The Victorians, chin-high in prudery, and the Edwardians, fast being emancipated, had anxieties enough; but they never knew the evil of economic inflation or of the Nuclear Threat. They blessedly had no notion even of world war. Stricter class divisions at least proffered the almost certain guarantee that the rich would stay rich and the poor would probably die prematurely. So what was the point of living in fear of a downward spiral on the one hand or of aspiring to wealth on the other?

The blend of usually well-bred amateurs with from-the-masses professionals worked well in county and Test cricket. The commander-in-chief was always from amateur ranks, carefree, uninhibited in tactical matters. His livelihood was not dependent upon success on the cricket field. He was often trained to lead, and elicited the respect of his men. (The egalitarian Australian system, while not free of the occasional squabble, worked well for them.) Then, the amateurs could afford to play for months at a time, and to sail off during the winter to some outpost of Empire, there to show that it was not only the waves that Britannia ruled. Now, three-quarters of a century on, the complex pressures of making a living, whether real or part-illusory, leave only humble weekend club cricketers free to play purely for fun.

The worship of Mammon has much – no, *everything*

– to answer for: the avarice that causes man to devote all his days to material acquisition and the greed that lures nations into war. The First World War exploded under cricket's Golden Age, and much else. It left a world which the late J.B. Priestley averred 'could never again be trusted'.

There is barely anyone left now who can describe first-hand how Ranji moved and what J.T. Hearne did with the ball and what effect W.G.'s bulky entrance into the field had on the gathering. We can go on reading contemporary accounts and studying photographs and drawings. And we can now also rejoice in the latest time-cheating phenomenon, Gerry Wright's resurrection work with canvas and paintbrush. Immersed in his beloved collection of old books and pictures, he says, with appropriate bashfulness, that he feels like some Grand Creator as he breathes life into old photographs. He gives them colour and vitality, an extra dimension. Not only that: he has brought an authenticity to his mission by consultations with archivists at Lord's and Melbourne, and by studying old pattern-books from the outfitters who manufactured those rainbow blazers nearly a century ago. The extra demands of complex colour-mixing have not affected his natural cheerfulness.

The limited practice of contemplating ancient monochromes, if not past, should at least move over. The new computer process of imposing colour on the old Hollywood movies has a counterpart in cricket. As you look upon the cricketers of old brought back to life, there is a dispensation for letting past your lips the wry verse of E.E. Bowen:

There were wonderful giants of old, you know,
There were wonderful giants of old;
They grew more mightily, all of a row,
Than ever was heard or told;
All of them stood their six-feet-four,
And they threw to a hundred yards or more,
And never were lame or stiff or sore;
And we, compared to the days of yore,
Are cast in a pigmy mould.

Guildford, 1985   DAVID FRITH

The Australians, 1899

The resurgence by Australia as the nineteenth century neared its end was maintained during their 1899 tour of England. In thirty-five first-class matches they forced sixteen victories and lost only to Essex, Surrey and Kent. By now, Test matches had taken on a giant importance, and this was the first series of five in England – all played over three days, with Australia triumphing by ten wickets at Lord's in the only Test to reach a finish. This game saw two momentous milestones. W.G. Grace, now fifty, was dropped from the England XI ('I can still bat but I can't bend'); and Victor Trumper, a last-minute enlistment for the tour, went in at number six and scored an unbeaten 135 with all the daring and beauty which were to raise his name to a sacred rarity. If this setting is Elysium, then there is a certainty among cricket-lovers that this is where the spirit of Trumper was bound upon his death in 1915, when he was only thirty-seven. He stands on the left, beside the lofty Hugh Trumble, who performed the 'double' of a thousand runs and a hundred wickets on this tour as well as holding forty-nine catches. Next comes Alf Johns, the reserve wicketkeeper, and Bill Howell, a beekeeper from New South Wales who buzzed through Surrey in his first outing, taking all ten wickets for 28 with medium-pace off-spinners. Ben Wardill, in the ten-gallon hat, managed the side, and Monty Noble, on his left, came close to the double, though he is better remembered this summer for having bowled the ball which Albert Trott smote over the high Lord's pavilion. Frank Laver had a quiet tour. A dozen years later he was to become embroiled in one of the costliest demonstrations of player power. Charlie McLeod, at the end of the line, was one of a talented Melbourne brotherhood. Seated are Jim Kelly, the wicketkeeper, a suitably bluff forebear of Rod Marsh; Clem Hill, the brilliant young left-hander; Jack Worrall, destined to give more with the pen than the bat; Joe Darling, the mighty left-hander, skipper for the first of three UK tours; Frank Iredale, a thoughtful batsman from Sydney; and Ernie Jones, the first great Australian fast bowler. Had he been to Prince Alfred College? enquired a member of the Royal Family. 'Yeah, I've driven the dust-cart up there,' replied 'Jonah'. In front squats Syd Gregory, a perennial tourist.

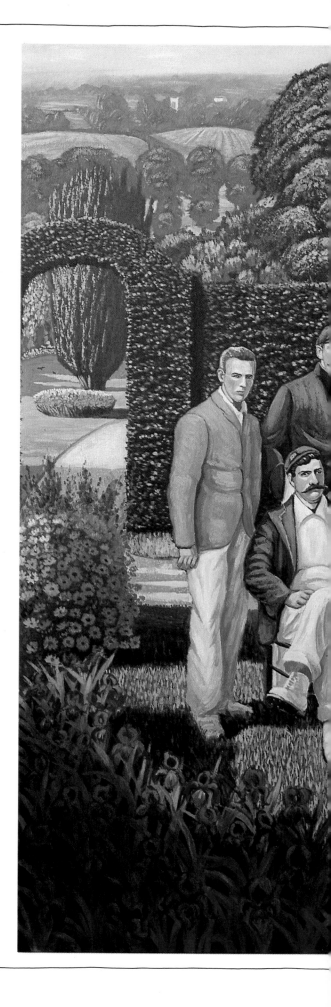

L.C.H. PALAIRET

THE NAME WAS as elegant as that of an ancient knight of honour: Lionel Charles Hamilton Palairet. The man's style was fitting too, the bat serving as a lance without any undue fits of fancy. Languid eyelids, languid bat, Pollock-style. Champagne, symbol of the debonair. Palairet graced teams of Repton schoolboys, Oxford undergraduates, the *pot-pourri* that was the Somerset XI, and, twice, England, though he failed each time at the ultimate level, which would have caused anguish to his father, who had been champion archer of all England. But L.C.H. once made 292 against Hampshire at Southampton, and raised a record 346 against Yorkshire for his county's first wicket with Herbert Tremenheere Hewett at Taunton in 1892; he was a noted middle-distance runner, and played football for the Corinthians, where his innate sense of chivalry would have responded to the code that a penalty kick won should be booted over the crossbar and a penalty conceded should be allowed to enter the net.

BILL LOCKWOOD

TOM RICHARDSON's name usually sprang first to the lips, but his Surrey and England fast-bowling partner, Bill Lockwood, was every bit as great a player. He was also a top-class batsman. But a tinge of perversity about his character created flaws in his performance, and his reputation is uneven in the comprehension of later generations. In form, and when he applied himself wholeheartedly, Lockwood bowled as challengingly as any bowler ever known. While Richardson was the tireless thunderer, Lockwood was master of the well-concealed slow ball, his stock delivery being a wicked breakback which could deceive even Shrewsbury – who first recommended him to Surrey when, a young lacemaker, he languished in Nottinghamshire's Club and Ground side. Equally dangerously, Lockwood generated devilish lift, the product of a good physique harnessed to a smooth action. In 1892 the world took notice when he became the most potent bowler in the nation with 151 wickets at less than fourteen apiece. Pitches at The Oval then were more dubious than when 'Bosser' Martin was to turn them into bowlers' nightmares, and visiting batsmen in the 1890s offered a quiet prayer before going out to face Lockwood and Richardson – and Lohmann. Lockwood went into eclipse for a season or two, and disappointed on his tour of Australia, in 1894–95; but he came back strong at thirty, took 7 for 71 in the 1899 Oval Test against Australia, and continued to be a force until retirement in 1904, two years after taking eleven Australian wickets in the celebrated Old Trafford Test, which England lost by three runs. If tragedy seems to stalk the period, Lockwood was another not to be spared. In 1896 he lost his wife and a child. He died in 1932, crippled by arthritis, but having had the joy of seeing Larwood, the latest Notts fast-bowling sensation, in action. Was he the best? 'There'll never be another Tom Richardson,' he said. Was Tom really better than Lockwood himself? 'I was never in the same parish.'

BILL LOCKWOOD

Rest of England XI, 1901

REMOVED INTO THIS garden paradise are the eleven who represented a Rest of England team at Lord's in 1901, a match in which the champions, Yorkshire, had to suffer defeat by an innings. The causes? The chap in the blue blazer, arms folded: C.B. Fry, who scored what was his sixth century in a row, then a world record; the little fellow in the back row, the great Jessop himself, who smote 233 runs in well under three hours; and Albert Trott, in the blue cap, next to him, who swerved, spun and yorked five batsmen out in the first innings and eight in the second. So much for the first Champion County v The Rest contest, which raised £350 for the widow of William Yardley, the Cambridge and Kent player. The combination which brought down the triumphant Tykes in the season's September twilight comprised: back row – Richard Brooks, a fine amateur wicket-keeper, Trott, Jessop, and George Wilson, Worcestershire fast bowler; seated – A.O. Jones, captain of Nottinghamshire and a future England captain, P.F. Warner of Middlesex, whose lifelong devotion to the game still had over sixty years to run, H.D.G. Leveson Gower – 'Shrimp' – whose pleasure at leading the Rest to victory was dampened for having been bowled by Hirst for a duck, G.W. Beldam, whose graphic action photography gave eternal life to so many Edwardian cricketers, and C.B. Fry, whose feat of six consecutive hundreds stood alone until Bradman and then Procter equalled, but did not surpass, it. In front are John Gunn, of the illustrious family of Nottinghamshire professionals, and Jimmy Sinclair, the lofty South African, who topped the South Africans' bowling averages on their tour that summer and walloped a Test century against Australia at Cape Town in only eighty minutes a year later.

CAMBRIDGE XI, 1895

T HE DAZZLING ARRAY of club blazers for once leaves Nature behind. Like a window-box of prize antirrhinums, the young cricketers of Cambridge University, 1895, either anticipate or reflect upon their comfortable victory over Oxford at Lord's with decorum and sanguine countenance. All these bar E.B. Shine, standing extreme right, played in the Varsity match. In Shine's place, W.G. Grace junior played, bringing joy to his father in what was his own most glorious year by scoring 40 and 28; which was just as well, for a year later, in the amateur event of the year, he was out twice without scoring, causing the great Doctor much pain. Shine, the odd man out in the group, achieved a notoriety of his own in that 1896 match by bowling three balls to the boundary in order to deny Oxford the compulsory follow-on. Such is the course of evolution of cricket's Laws. For once, a pre-Great War group may not be singled out for the tragic casualties that lay ahead. None from this team perished in the First World War. Indeed, their average age when the lifespan of the last had run its course was seventy-three. Of the back row – W.W. Lowe, J. Burrough, W.M. Hemingway, E.B. Shine – Hemingway had the longest real-life innings at ninety-three. Of those seated – H. Gray, F. Mitchell, W.G. Druce, N.F. Druce, R.A. Studd – W.G. Druce, the captain, reached ninety. On the moistureless grass in front sit H.H. Marriott and C.E.M. Wilson. Three of the team entered the Church, two – N.F. Druce and Wilson – played for England (and Studd had two brothers who did), and Frank Mitchell, Yorkshire-born, played cricket and rugby for England, served in the Boer War, and captained South Africa on two tours of his homeland.

ARTHUR SHREWSBURY

Arthur Shrewsbury

Knee-deep in poppies, with their connotations of tragedy, symbolically stands Arthur Shrewsbury, the little Nottinghamshire master of batsmanship, about whom W.G. Grace remarked, when asked who was the best batsman of all (himself naturally excluded): 'Give me Arthur!' Shrewsbury's defence was little short of impregnable, based on limitless patience and a ready willingness to pad the ball away in days when only the straight ball could result in a leg-before-wicket decision. He was a professional through and through, and even ventured into the promotion of tours – cricket and rugby – with Notts friend and team-mate Alfred Shaw. His name, though, lives on for the skill which proclaimed him as the finest professional batsman in England, and therefore the world, for several years up to the early 1890s, a high skill never better displayed than during his innings of 164 on a dangerous pitch in the Test against Australia at Lord's in 1886. There, he held off the spiteful assault of Spofforth, 'The Demon', and a flush of five other top-class bowlers for seven hours. Curiously, Shrewsbury travelled uneasily, and was seldom comfortable in a strange bed. Another peculiarity was his sensitivity about his baldness: he was rarely seen without a cap on his global head. Convinced that he had a terminal illness, Arthur Shrewsbury, a bachelor, shot himself in 1903. He was forty-seven.

Woolley and Hutchings

At the outbreak of the Great War, Kenneth Hutchings's career was ostensibly over, though he was only thirty-one, while Frank Woolley's had a long way to go. Hutchings, the amateur, became a lieutenant in the King's Liverpool Regiment, and was blown apart by a shell in France. Woolley (on the chair), the professional, twenty-seven at the start of hostilities, joined the Royal Navy, survived, played on for county and country until he was fifty-one, and left figures of staggering dimensions in the record books: just under 60,000 runs, 145 centuries, over 2,000 wickets, and a world record 1,018 catches. It was one of sporting life's rich experiences to see Hutchings and Woolley batting together for Kent. Woolley, the left-hander, willowy and calm, compulsively aggressive, his swirling bat something like a wand, used with the same apparent languor seen in the batting of David Gower, who played his first Test a few months before Woolley died in 1978, in his ninety-second year. Hutchings, bareheaded, suntanned, built his elegant game on daring driving. He sought to hit every ball through what the

modern player would call the 'V' – unless he was reluctantly forced to play back. His cavalier batsmanship had much to do with Kent's first-ever County Championship, in 1906, and a year later, in Australia, he stroked a century at Melbourne which remains one of the classics of Test cricket. Hutchings and Woolley in partnership while Edward VII was king – the tang of hops, the beauty of roses, the sad poignancy of lilies.

THE PLAYERS, 1895

THE BIG MATCH of the season, the occasional Test series notwithstanding, was the Gentlemen v Players fixture, specifically the one at Lord's. The Players – the professionals – won the 1895 match after setting the Gentlemen 336 to win and dismissing them for 303, Bobby Peel and Tom Richardson (in his first such game) taking seven wickets each and Albert Ward (76), Bill Storer (93), Peel (71 not out) and Richardson (43) all making important second-innings runs. Tom Hayward, who was also making his debut in this show event, scored 60 in the first innings. The Players brought to life from the old photograph are (standing) Bobby Abel, the little Surrey batsman; Arthur Mold, a Lancashire fast bowler who came off the pitch with great force, but who became deeply disenchanted when no-balled for throwing; William Attewell, a stoic Nottinghamshire bowler whose reputation for accuracy was unmatched; and Bobby Peel, the clever Yorkshire slow-medium left-arm bowler who liked a drink more than most. Seated are Albert Ward of Lancashire, a fine batsman who did conspicuously well for England more than once; Tom Richardson, the brave and tireless Surrey fast bowler, born in a gipsy caravan; William Gunn, the captain, an exceptionally tall player, a founder of the Gunn & Moore batmaking company, and legendary Nottinghamshire partner of Shrewsbury; Frank Sugg, a powerful batsman who played for three counties, principally for Lancashire, and excelled at half a dozen sports; and Tom Hayward, of Surrey, who was to go on to become only the second batsman to register a hundred centuries. In front are George Davidson, a Derbyshire bowler who died young and left an impoverished family, and Bill Storer, Derbyshire's wicketkeeper, an outspoken character who often batted well and even took his turn at the bowling crease. The decisive factor in these traditional matches was the depth of the professionals' bowling. In 1895, at Lord's, they had four world-class bowlers in Richardson, Peel, Mold and Attewell, which made W.G.'s century, his last at Lord's, all the more laudable.

J.R. MASON

I N A SETTING as pretty as Kent itself in full bloom sits Jack Mason, captain of the county, six-foot-plus allrounder, perhaps looking slightly hangdog at the recall of running out W.G. in the Gentlemen v Players match at Lord's in 1899, trying for a quick single and overlooking his partner's fifty-one years and inhibiting bulk. Mason was an early-model Hammond: straight-batted, upright, with a magnificent drive and cut, and not only a top-class fast-medium bowler but a wonderfully adroit slip fieldsman as well. Unlike the Gloucestershire player of the next generation, Mason played little for his country. His tour of Australia with Stoddart in 1897-98 produced only 129 runs in the five Tests, and he was

never chosen for a home Test match – although he was among the fourteen summoned to Edgbaston in 1902. Educated at Winchester, he qualified as a solicitor and played little from his early thirties because of the demands of his profession. Through his office window he must often have dispatched his spirit to the sunlit fields.

CHARLES KORTRIGHT

SUCCESSIVE GENERATIONS have never quite understood how Kortright should have been regarded as the most feared of fast bowlers, and yet never played for England. Contemporaries are not to be mistrusted. They are almost as one in saying that 'Korty' was the quickest of the lot. Tall, strong and athletic, he cantered in twenty yards and let fly a ball of such velocity that he must be compared with Larwood and Holding, if not with Tyson. P.F. Warner said he was extremely fast through the air, but did not come off the pitch with corresponding speed. That is one for the professors of physics. What is known is that during the late 1890s he had competition from Richardson, Lockwood and Mold – all professionals – and, like a fast bowler or two of more recent years, he was temperamental. An amateur, he had private means and seldom seemed to need to work. Under a scorching Australian sun, a bowler who would give his all, and more, was needed; and that is probably why captains chose to take professionals like Richardson, Hearne and Hirst on their tours. Kortright's speed was potent, nevertheless, for he prompted Abel to say, 'I am the father of thirteen children and there are plenty of other bowlers to make runs off.' He flinched at Lord's, but got even on the hard Oval pitch with a century against Essex. Kortright was uncompromising, and even precipitated a feud with the fearsome W.G. And in a club match at Wallingford he became so irked that he bounced one clean over the sightscreen for six byes.

B.J.T. Bosanquet

Bernard James Tindal Bosanquet – 'Bosie' – of Oxford, Middlesex and England, was shrewd enough to realise that there were more comfortable ways of spending a hot afternoon than tearing in to bowl fast on a shirtfront pitch upon which batsmen could play with ease. So he developed the 'googly', the ball which spins the 'wrong' way, from off to leg, even though it appears to be delivered with a leg-break action. After years of experiment, he began to 'walk slowly up to the wicket and gently propel the ball into the air' in important matches. The process was hardly gentle. Bemused batsmen played in one direction as the ball spun in another, and dark murmurings circulated at the chap's effrontery in 'cheating' in this way. Certainly, for a time, he was happy to let everyone believe that the freak balls were somehow accidentally created. But the truth soon established itself. 'With a silent prayer' he turned his wrist over, whipped a googly down at Trumper, the Australian genius, and tilted his middle stump backwards. Sometimes his control left much to be desired, the ball bouncing three or four times. But he was brave enough to persist, backed by understanding captains. And in Australia, in 1903–04, when barrackers on the Hill at Sydney called him 'Elsie' because of his colourful sweater, he tore through the opposition with six for 51 as England recaptured the Ashes. A year later, back in England, he took eight for 107 to spin out Australia in the Trent Bridge Test match, increasing his popularity – and that of his invention – immeasurably. But decline soon came, and he concentrated thereafter on his batting, leaving his imaginative innovation to be exploited by an international chain of exponents from Schwarz, Mailey, Freeman, Grimmett and O'Reilly to Wright, Dooland, Benaud, Chandrasekhar, Abdul Qadir, Sivaramakrishnan. . . .

A Club Team

REPRESENTING THE MASSES of anonymous cricketers who played every weekend in boyish escape from the drudgery of work: a village team, often the amalgam of landed gentry, clergy, publican, blacksmith and schoolboy, but here seen as a band of artisans, the fresh smell of the woodlands sweet in their nostrils. With a flannel shirt costing six-and-eleven, white mock-buck spiked boots eight-and-eleven, and shrunk white flannels seven-and-eleven, what was the point in wasting hard-earned money? And as for a bat, a 'Guv'nor' from Bobby Abel's shop up in Kennington Road would cost sixteen-and-eleven; and think how many days' food supply that represented. Anyway, there is something nice about using one of the communal bats, even if it is for only a few minutes every Saturday afternoon. The importance of the scorer's book cannot be over-emphasised, even if it has long since turned to dust.

LORD SHEFFIELD'S XI

.G. GRACE VISITED AUSTRALIA only twice. The first tour, in 1873-74, became his 'honeymoon' tour, with a sizable pay-packet to go with it. Though never other than an 'amateur' on the surface, he continued to rake in the money for appearances, and Lord Sheffield was bound to come up with an enticing offer to get him to the Colonies in 1891. His fee was £3,000, and his family accompanied him. But the series was lost two-one, and the Doctor managed only two half-centuries in his five Test innings. The voyages to and from Australia were long and often rough, and travel internally was an endurance test; and although the experience was enthralling in so many ways, with bush sport and adventure there for the taking and games against teams of twenty or so minor cricketers providing easy runs and wickets, it was always – and has been since

– a relief to return to the English garden ... and, in this canvas, English umpires (Carpenter and Thoms). Each of these players had some success to look back upon, none more so than Bobby Abel (seated right), who carried his bat for 132 through England's innings in the Sydney Test, and A.E. Stoddart (next to Abel), who hit a sound and attractive 134 in the Adelaide Test, which was won. Here, Johnny Briggs, the little Lancashire left-arm spinner (seated left), took twelve wickets in the match, while the Yorkshire left-hander, Bobby Peel (next to Stoddart), made his highest Test score of 83. Between Briggs and Grace sits Gregor MacGregor, the wicketkeeper, who also played rugby for Scotland. The five hardy professionals at the back are William Attewell, George Lohmann, who took eight for 58 in Australia's first innings in the Sydney Test, Maurice Read, George Bean and Jack Sharpe, who, lacking a right eye, always preferred to present a left profile to the camera.

WILFRED RHODES

I
N HIS NINETY-SIXTH and last year, Wilfred Rhodes, blind for over a decade, could still recount with clarity incidents from his long playing career, which began in 1898. The tales were burnished through retelling and from an analytical mind, a mind which controlled the fingers of a cunning left hand which lured 4,187 batsmen to their doom, a tally unapproached in cricket history. Twenty-three times he took a hundred or more wickets in a season, and he gained much amusement from moving from number eleven in the England batting order to number one – two, perhaps, for he had ungrudging admiration for his partner, the southern-born Jack Hobbs. If he looks slightly ill at ease in the Arcadian setting, it must be remembered that he spent half his summer days and many of his winters around smoky Sheffield and bricky Bradford and humble Huddersfield.

'TIBBY' COTTER

I N AN AGE WHEN fast bowlers did not hunt in pairs – much less foursomes – Albert 'Tibby' Cotter from Sydney stood alone as a tearaway slinger of high pace, in the Jeff Thomson mould, a stump-splitter and rib-cracker. He took over a hundred wickets on the 1905 tour of England, and his jousts with MacLaren and Hayward and Jackson were among the grand spectacles of the day. He was the perfect athlete, clear-skinned and clear-minded, broad of shoulder, fleet of foot. Joining up with the Australian 12th Light Horse, he missed guard duty in order to join in the charge on Beersheba in October 1917. There he was gunned down by a Turk, one of whose number he had claimed the day before. He had had a premonition. Tossing a ball of mud into the air, he said to a mate: 'That's my last bowl, Blue. Something's going to happen.'

J.N. Crawford and R.E. Foster

CRAWFORD AND FOSTER

THE QUESTION BEGS an answer: was there ever as much skill and artistry bound up in a pair of cricketers as in J.N. Crawford and R.E. Foster? Their fame was not the kind that hovers, cliché-like, for generations to come, for in Crawford's case he walked out on the English game after a dispute with Surrey in 1909 and spent the next few years in Adelaide; and in Foster's case he was unable to afford the time to play for more than one full season or to go on more than one overseas tour. He featured in no more than 112 first-class matches, Crawford in 210. And Crawford spread his career over three countries: England, Australia and New Zealand. Not that their paths crossed. Jack Crawford, in his chocolate Surrey blazer, had made his debut for the county at seventeen, while still at Repton. A year later he sailed to South Africa with Warner's MCC team, and in 1906 and 1907 he completed the double – and narrowly missed it in 1908, the summer of his 232 against Somerset at The Oval. It was also a time when the Oval fans could bask in the joy of watching the brilliant first phase of Jack Hobbs's career. In the last southern summer before the Great War, the bespectacled Crawford toured New Zealand with an Australian combination, and indulged with Trumper in one of the most spectacular pieces of hitting ever seen. Against Fifteen of Canterbury at Temuka, Crawford smashed 354 in five and a half hours, with fourteen sixes and forty-five fours, adding 298 for the eighth wicket with Trumper in only sixty-nine minutes. Two months later, as chance would have it, the cricket world's attention was diverted to the shock news that 'Tip' Foster, who had played his last match two years earlier, was dead at thirty-six, victim of diabetes. Foster, here resplendent in I Zingari colours, had scored two centuries for Worcestershire against Hampshire in 1899 in a match in which his brother Wilfrid had done likewise. (Seven Foster brothers played for the county.) In 1900 he made two centuries at Lord's for the Gentlemen against the Players. Most memorably, though, he scored 287 at Sydney in his first Test match, a record destined to stand for ages. An England soccer cap, he led his country at cricket in 1907 against South Africa. A batsman of all imaginable style, Foster, in A.C. MacLaren's words, 'satisfied the public's longing for the picturesque in sport'.

HORNBY AND BARLOW

O MY HORNBY AND MY BARLOW LONG AGO! The most poignant and oft-paraphrased verse in cricket was penned by the tortured and doomed Lancastrian poet and essayist Francis Thompson, whose degradation in London touched such depths that he was refused admission to the public libraries, so ragged was his appearance. Sustained by the support of Wilfrid Meynell, editor of *Merry England*, Thompson, haggard from undernourishment and his addiction to opium, continued to pen his dark poetry, 'At Lord's', based on memories of a Lancashire v Gloucestershire match at Old Trafford in 1878, enduring into immortality. *And I look through my tears on a soundless-clapping host / As the run-stealers flicker to and fro*: 'Monkey' Hornby, the gaily-attired amateur, captain of England at rugby and cricket, an attacking batsman, as befitted a positive personality; and Dick Barlow, the professional, dour to the point of exasperation to spectators and opponents, eyes cool, spade beard defiant. Twice he 'existed' at the crease for two and a half hours for a paltry five runs, and in a Test match against Australia he scored 90 in almost six hours, inspiring *Punch* to launch into satirical verse. Hornby was always of more heroic stuff. When Lord Harris was attacked by a mob who invaded the field at Sydney, 'Monkey', the redoubtable international rugby three-quarter, moved to His Lordship's assistance and dragged away one particularly obnoxious ruffian, though he took a blow to the face and had his shirt ripped from his back. Hornby and Barlow harmonised, though they were almost opposites – their ratio of run-scoring around ten to one – and the latter came close to matching the poet Thompson in sentimentality, for his house was filled with trophies and mementoes from a cricket career which covered many years and countless miles.

FRONTISPIECE ILLUSTRATION

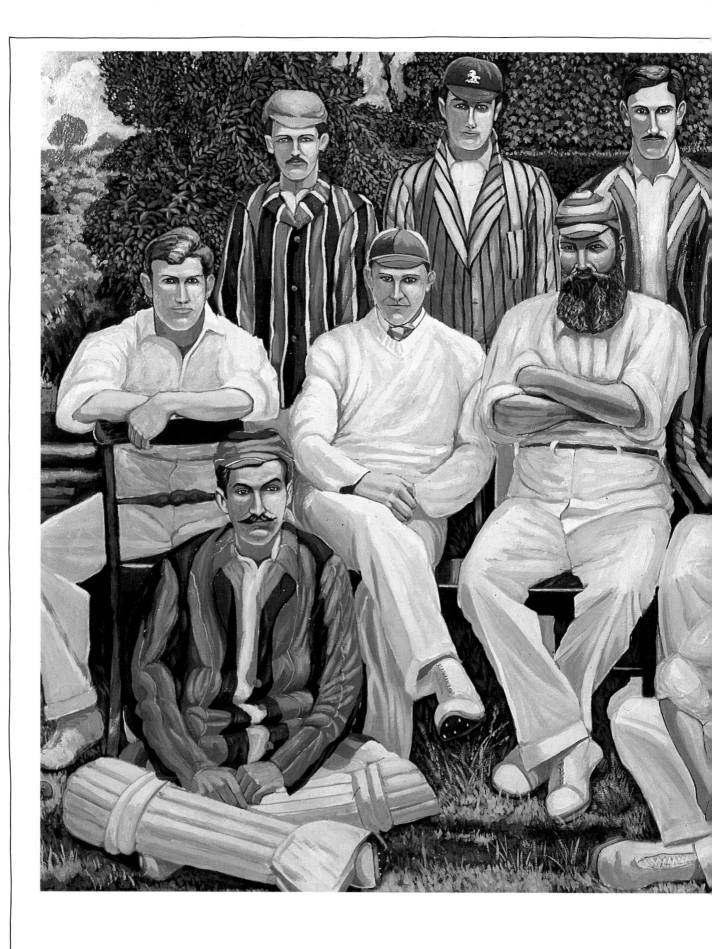

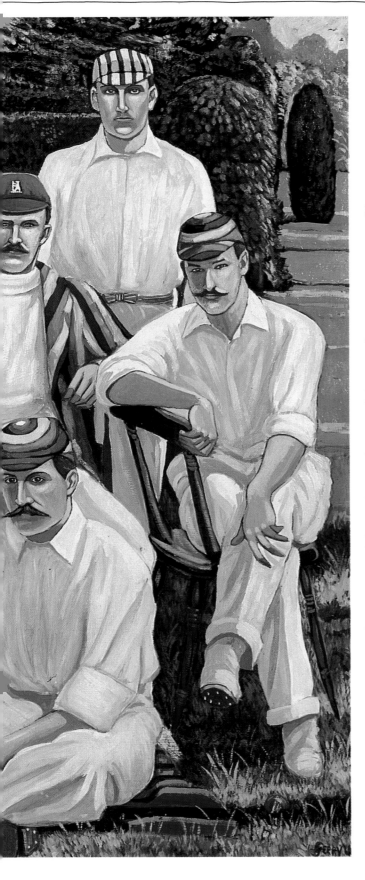

THE GENTLEMEN, 1894

THE GREAT BEARDED figure of Dr W.G. Grace presides over the Gentlemen's XI at Lord's in 1894. Already nearer fifty than forty, W.G. pleased everyone by making 56 against an impressive professional line-up. And yet his greatest triumph lay a year ahead, when he was to reach a thousand runs before May was out and notch his hundredth century, feats hailed nationally with wonder and jubilation. Here, in 1894, he led his side to victory by an innings, F.S. Jackson scoring 63 and then bowling through both of the Players' innings unchanged with Sammy Woods, Jackson taking twelve wickets, Woods six. Standing in the group are James Douglas, a handsome Middlesex batsman; J.R. Mason, an upstanding Kent batsman; G.J. Mordaunt, also of Kent – and Oxford – a strokemaker who was also magnificent in the field; and A.C. MacLaren, a Golden Age favourite, superior in style and manner, fiery in attitude as well as strokeplay. Seated are S.M.J. Woods, Australian-born rugby-playing allrounder, whose play was as rumbustious as any to be seen in any age; H.T. Hewett, hard-hitting left-hander, Somerset skipper, co-owner (with Palairet) of the county's first-wicket record of 346; W.G. Grace, the most recognisable male figure in England, with the possible exception only of Gladstone; H.W. Bainbridge, stern-faced Warwickshire captain; and the Honourable F.S. Jackson, man of huge accomplishment, not only on the cricket field: a cultured, chivalrous Yorkshireman, he was a Member of Parliament, Governor of Bengal – and Winston Churchill was his fag at Harrow. In front are Gregor MacGregor, Scottish rugby international and Middlesex and England wicketkeeper, and his flatmate, A.E. Stoddart, stylish Middlesex opening batsman, who was about to lead an English team to Australia in one of the most enthralling of all Test series. Much of the cream of amateur batsmanship of the 1890s is here; to refer to many of them by christian names rather than initials even now seems to border on impertinence.

G.L. JESSOP

G. L. JESSOP

He stands innocently midst the aromatic flowers. They would more aptly be stinging-nettles. 'Jessopus' – Gilbert Laird Jessop – maintained a startling success rate as an incurably belligerent batsman. Only five feet seven inches in height, he crouched at the crease like an Edwardian mugger in wait for a wealthy-looking victim. The problem for bowlers of even the highest class was that Jessop, with his sharp eye, catlike reflexes and great strength, aimed to hit everything bowled at him for four (there were no sixes before 1910, unless the ball was hit clean out of the ground: and Jessop partook of much more than an average slice of that predilection). Centuries in an hour or less came with unique frequency from his bludgeon of a bat as this demon intimidated and exasperated Gloucestershire's opposing bowlers. His hundred for England against Australia, at The Oval in 1902, is on the short-list of 'greatest innings of all'. Needing 263 to win, England were half out for only 48. In a frantic hour and a quarter, split by the tea interval, Jessop smote Trumble and Saunders all over the ground to bring England back into the game. One spectator, young bank clerk P.G. Wodehouse, thought the tall Trumble's off-breaks were close to unplayable. Hirst and Rhodes ensured that Jessop's effort was not wasted. They got England home with a wicket to spare. Jessop was less than an overall success in Test cricket, though he loved the stimulation of the ultimate competition. But with his strike rate of 79 runs an hour he slaughtered bad- and good-length bowling alike, up and down England, always with a sense of humour, typified by the gift of lettuce-leaves which he sent to a Worcestershire fast bowler after crashing 49 runs off him in three overs. The bowler had let it be known that he considered Jessop to be his 'rabbit'. That was like threatening to outdraw Billy the Kid.

S. F. BARNES

The lion in repose. Tall and gaunt, Sydney Francis Barnes, perhaps the greatest bowler of all time, looks harmless enough knee-deep in flowers, but once he had the ball in his long, strong fingers, no batsman was safe. He spun it at the top side of medium pace and with unerring control.

Lifetime figures in all competitive cricket of over six thousand wickets at eight apiece tell a significant part of the story. That he chose to spend most of his summers – and well beyond middle age at that – in Minor County and league cricket is explained not by a desire to gobble up minnows but rather by a near-fanatical need to capitalise on his talent financially. He played only twenty-seven times for England, and yet pocketed 189 wickets: seven per match. In South Africa, on the matting wickets of 1913–14, when he was forty, he was almost unplayable: he took 49 wickets in four Tests. But he is best remembered for a sensational spell one morning at Melbourne in 1911, when, laced with whisky to combat heavy 'flu, he whisked out five Australians for six runs. MacLaren had drawn the Staffordshire man out of obscurity and taken him to Australia the first time in 1901. He was still knocking wickets over in the Lancashire League forty years later. The flowers might well serve to mark batsmen's graves.

P.F. WARNER

P. F. WARNER

I F EVER A CRICKETER belonged to Lord's it was 'Plum' Warner. He batted there for his school, Rugby, his university, Oxford, his county, Middlesex, his 'class', the Gentlemen, and for his country. Though born in Port-of-Spain, the eighteenth child of the sixty-seven-year-old Attorney-General of Trinidad, who married twice, Warner became a symbol of English cricket. This is not to say that he was parochial, for, in an expansive age, no cricketer showed more enthusiasm for taking the game to the furthest-flung shores, even beyond the Empire. Indeed, he carried a tattered MCC flag with him on many of his travels, a relic of two successful tours of Australia, in the second of which, in 1911–12, ill-health kept him from the field after the opening match. He was never robust, yet he lived on until his ninetieth year, dying, almost symbolically, just as amateur status, with all the humbug that went with it, was being abolished. Boyish in appearance until the last, he sits in his colourful dream surroundings, Harlequin cap atop, oblivious of the grievous episode ahead, when, as MCC's manager in Australia with Jardine's ruthless fast-bowling company, he proved powerless to influence England's captain against tactics which jeopardised Anglo-Australian relations. Surviving to yet another generation, and another, Pelham Francis Warner wrote and selected and presided, and was knighted in 1937 for services to cricket. His ashes were scattered at Lord's in front of the Warner Stand, where he had hit his first boundary on the great ground as a Rugby schoolboy.

The Australians, 1893

EMERGING FROM THE greyness of a photograph come the eighth Australian combination to tour England (excluding the 1868 Aborigines). The green caps and blazers, which were to become vividly emblematic in the twentieth century, represented here no more than an incipient unity, for it was not until 1 January 1901, Day 1 of the new century, that the States were to be joined in nationhood. Australia had lost the four Test series in England preceding the 1893 tour, and went down again in this one, losing the Oval Test by an innings. They also failed to make much impression in the county matches, though there was an abundance of talent in this line-up, some of it with the best years to come. Bracketed by the English umpires Carpenter and Thoms in the back row are Victor Cohen, the manager, Affie Jarvis, Walter Giffen, Billy Bruce and Alec Bannerman. Seated are Harry Trott, Hugh Trumble, George Giffen, Jack Blackham (captain), Jack Lyons, Bob McLeod and Charlie Turner. In front are Harry Graham, Arthur Coningham, and Syd Gregory. Blackham, ace of wicketkeepers, was on his eighth and final tour of England, Gregory on the second of eight tours: they sailed almost half a million miles between them. George Giffen, the 'W.G. of Australia', toured only when it was reluctantly accepted that his brother Walter, a much lesser cricketer, should be included in the side, a strange forerunner to Harry Trott's decision three years later *not* to bring his brother Albert, who was already one of the world's leading allrounders. The boyish Harry Graham made history when he scored a century at Lord's in his first Test innings, the first half of a unique double, for he scored another hundred at Sydney two years later in his first Test innings on home soil. Coningham, on the other hand, played in none of the 1893 Tests, and found the weather so disagreeable at Blackpool that he gathered litter, set light to it in the outfield, and warmed his fingers.

COLIN BLYTHE

COLIN BLYTHE, known to all and sundry as 'Charlie', was a hypersensitive Cockney with a sweet nature and an academic forehead which misled. An accomplished violinist, he spread his art to the cricket field with slow left-arm bowling, the variations upon which posed a ceaseless challenge to Kent's and England's opponents. Devastating on a damp pitch, he took ten for 30 and seven for 18 in one day against Northamptonshire in 1907, the year in which he also confounded South Africa with fifteen wickets in the Headingley Test match. The sustained mental effort of performances such as these, and when he took eleven wickets against Australia at Edgbaston two years later, left him mentally shattered. Retirement just before the Great War brought relief. His greatest sacrifice was yet to come, however, for, despite his dubious health (he was an epileptic), he enrolled in the Kent Fortress Engineers, made the rank of sergeant, and was killed near Passchendaele. His shrapnel-scarred wallet, taken from his body, is on display in Kent's museum at the St Lawrence Ground, Canterbury.

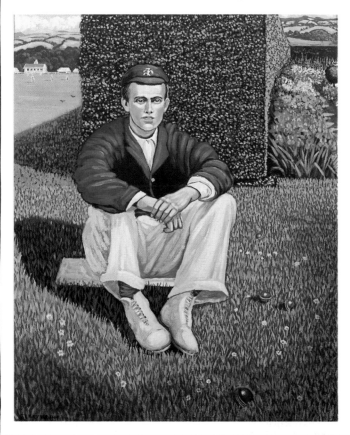

F.S. JACKSON AND WILFRED RHODES

YORKSHIRE CRICKET-LOVERS of the modern age, when the county club has been split into bitter factions and victory on the field has been a rare event, will reflect longingly upon the great days of yore, when, in spite of the amateur-professional division, the team exerted its might in a common direction. It is not by accident that the respective poses of the Honourable F.S. Jackson, seated elegantly, with debonair straw boater, and Wilfred Rhodes, the professional who was down to earth in life as well as literally in the painting, are as they are; and the bright beauty of their surroundings serves only further to haunt those who have witnessed the undignified controversies of Yorkshire in the Boycott era. Stanley Jackson was a classic Golden Age batsman – all powerful drives and cracking square-cuts – and a fine fast-medium bowler. He is remembered principally for his exploits in the 1905 Tests against Australia, when he captained England, won all five tosses, headed the batting, and won the series two-nil. While Jackson, whose life was full of so many public pursuits, gave only a portion of his time to cricket, Rhodes devoted a lifetime to it. (He died, now blind, in 1973, aged ninety-five.) In a long playing career, he took a world record 4,187 first-class wickets with cunning slow left-arm bowling, and worked his way up the batting order from England's number eleven to Jack Hobbs's opening partner, posting 323 with him at Melbourne in 1912. 'You've only got one shot!' taunted one of the Australians. 'That's all I need on this wicket,' murmured Wilfred imperturbably. Many of the amateurs who captained Yorkshire uttered their orders only after consultation with the wily Rhodes. He knew the game well, and the white rose of Yorkshire was engraved on his heart.

F.S. Jackson and Wilfred Rhodes

LANCASHIRE, 1894

WHERE ARE THE mills and chimneys? Where is the damp turf, the overcast sky? No War of the Roses here. Just twelve Lancashire cricketers true, nine professionals and three amateurs – Archie MacLaren, the skipper, seated centrally, with S. M. Tindall on his right and G. R. Bardswell, defying the moustache vogue, on his left. In front are Johnny Briggs, wicketkeeper Charlie Smith, and Alf Tinsley. Is it imagination that sees tragedy written across the wistful face of Briggs, the bouncy little joker who bobbed in to bowl his left-arm slows for county and country? Chosen at sixteen for his batting and brilliant cover fielding, he played for Lancashire for twenty-two years, taking over two thousand first-class wickets, 118 of them in Test matches, and many on his six tours of Australia and one to South Africa. He is still the only player with both a Test hat-trick and a Test century to his credit. Subject to epilepsy, he broke down several times in his last few years, and was sheltered in Cheadle Asylum, where he was often seen bowling an imaginary ball down the corridor to an imaginary batsman. He died in the institution in 1901, in his fortieth year. Of Briggs's other team-mates in the painting, Albert Ward, seated left, and Frank Sugg, seated right, were solid, high-scoring batsmen, while Arthur Paul, standing second from left, later coach at Old Trafford, had his memorable day when he added 363 for the second wicket with MacLaren at Taunton in 1895. MacLaren, still only twenty-two, hit 424 in just under eight hours – and sold a few evening papers. It remains the highest score ever recorded in England in a first-class match. To the right of the scorer, in his straw boater, are George Baker and Arthur Smith, and standing on the left is Arthur Mold, one of the most penetrative of fast bowlers, despite his short run to the wicket. He and Briggs carried the attack almost exclusively, no one else taking more than nine wickets that summer. Lancashire finished fourth this season, but were runners-up in both the following years, and became champions in 1897.

A.E. Stoddart

A.E. STODDART

ANDREW ERNEST STODDART – 'Drewy' or 'Stoddy' to his countless friends – has only recently emerged from the oblivion into which his enormous reputation was plunged for over half a century following his suicide in 1915. One of the supreme batsmen of the Golden Age, he led England on two tours of Australia in the 1890s, having toured twice before. There, he tightened up his batting in the team's interest, and achieved a score of 173 in a Melbourne Test which was to last eighty years as the highest by an England captain in Australia. His early fame came as England's outstanding rugby three-quarter, but a world record score of 485 for Hampstead in a club match against Stoics in 1886 and a flow of runs at that level and in county cricket for Middlesex established him in the top rank. Often he opened for England or the Gentlemen with W.G. Grace – and looked in no way inferior. Modest, stylish and free-spirited, he surprised many by preferring to play for his county instead of England in two Tests in 1890. Later in the decade, though, he earned immense fame and popularity as an England batsman, so soon to enter into tragic and lonely decline.

C.B. Fry and G.L. Jessop

Fry and Jessop

. B. FRY AND G. L. JESSOP were in contrast in so many different ways. Fry, almost too brilliant, in the allround sense, for his own good: cricketer, footballer, athlete, scholar, writer, editor, hunter, wit, naïve Nazi sympathiser, honorary naval captain, an Oxford man. Jessop was Cambridge, as unorthodox a batsman as Fry was devoted to the theory of technique. Their variance in orthodoxy tones well with their respective poses here: Fry properly seated, Jessop informally draped on the lawn. Their surnames were once regularly on the lips of thousands every day of the golden summers around the turn of the century, Jessop for his merciless hitting, Fry for his somewhat stiff but often massively successful batsmanship, so much of it in the company of Ranjitsinhji's dreamlike artistry for Sussex.

Warwick Armstrong

THEY CALLED HIM 'The Big Ship', for his dominant, uncompromising personality was matched by a physical bulk which grew annually, until he was a gargantuan twenty-one stone on his fourth tour of England, in 1921. One of his teammates referred to him as a 'mountain of meat'. His was unquestionably a threatening presence. Armstrong's value to Australia was as an allrounder – a powerful, sometimes stodgy, batsman of huge strength but no charm, though distinguished for his skill on wet pitches; and a nagging leg-spin bowler who turned little, rolling them in on leg stump and just outside, daring the batsman to take risks. He achieved the double on the 1905 and 1909 tours, and again in 1921, when he led Australia to a run of eight victories in a row over England. His bully image endeared him to few, and there were even members of his own Victoria and Australia sides who were, to say the least, wary of him. But he got the job done, and he was fearless, standing up to the 'aristocracy' at Lord's – including Lord Harris – by demanding free days before Test matches, and tuning up his own batsmen as a prime objective, even if it meant not enforcing the follow-on against a county. For long he cast a vast shadow over English cricket, and he is perhaps best remembered as the strokeplayer who made 303 not out against Somerset at Bath and 248 not out against the Gentlemen at Lord's on the 1905 tour.

A.C. MacLaren, K.S. Ranjitsinhji, Wilfred Rhodes

MacLaren, Ranjitsinhji, Rhodes

HERE IS AN INTERESTING juxtaposition: Mac-Laren, who always assumed the guise of lord and master; Ranji, truly a prince, though not as soon as some obsequious people had believed; and Rhodes, the archetypal professional, ripe with ideas though always subordinate. MacLaren bestrode the Golden Age, disdainful of much that went on around him, intent on personal success, scratching for money oft-times. His innings of 424 for Lancashire implanted his reputation with an awesomeness which never receded. His unearthing of S.F. Barnes from the obscurity of league cricket suggested he was a spotter of talent above the ordinary – although anyone seeing what Barnes could do with a cricket ball might safely have backed him for higher honours. And when, in 1921, he got together a team to beat Armstrong's all-conquering Australians in a match at Eastbourne, MacLaren was hailed as an Englishman far beyond the norm. Which he was. As for Ranji, who learned his cricket at Cambridge, he may have been an Indian, but England – and indeed Australia, until he criticised it – regarded him with a special warmth. Had he not been exotic because of his colour and background, still he would have thrilled the thousands by the sweep of his bat and the magical dominance he cast over the opposition bowling. Archie and Ranji, princes of the crease. Wilfred Rhodes, pre-eminent among the slow bowlers, almost all of them professionals, flighting the leather sphere, generously civil if not servile in response to the amateurs' success, gratified almost beyond words when the mighty drive following the boundary hit finished up in long-off's hands.

OXFORD PAST AND PRESENT, 1899

THEY CAME FROM Winchester, Repton and Eton, Wellington, Marlborough and Tonbridge. Some were still 'up', while others had departed Oxford University already for the wider world, three (Cunliffe, Lewis and Forbes) to die in the conflicts in South Africa and Europe. In June of 1899 they played and lost to the Australians – not here in the leafy elegance of The Parks but at the United Services' Ground, Portsmouth, C.B. Fry having just played in the Test match at Lord's, won by Australia. One team member is missing – perhaps he took the original photograph – but of the Eleven, the most renowned players are in the front row: Alec Eccles, who batted for Lancashire until 1907; George Fitz-Hardinge Berkeley, who had the glad memory of figures of eight for 72 with his left-arm seamers against the 1890 Australians; H.D.G. Leveson Gower, an influential amateur who went on to captain Surrey and, on the 1909–10 tour of South Africa, England; C.B. Fry, a sporting and intellectual giant in this and most other contexts; and F.H.E. Cunliffe, another left-arm medium-pacer, who was good enough to take eight for 26 against Surrey. A baronet and military historian, ironically he was one of the war casualties.

Ranjitsinhji and Woods

Ranji and 'sam', two of the golden favourites of English cricket-watchers, though neither was born in England. The Indian prince was the essence of gentility and grace, while the rugged S.M.J. Woods was born near Sydney, educated at Brighton College, and became resident at Cambridge, though no scholar was he. Woods was a bold batsman, no delicacy to watch, and a fast low-armed slinger who once took all ten for his University against C.I. Thornton's XI. He was also a key figure in the Somerset sides of the 1890s which were often an easy touch for the bigger counties, though they did succeed in upturning mighty Yorkshire on more than one surprise occasion. Sam, who liked to breakfast on lobsters and champagne, with a fat cigar to complicate the taste, played for both England and Australia, and also won thirteen England rugby caps as a rampaging wing forward. Like Bill Alley so many years later, Woods, though born far away, was accepted as one of Somerset's own, and his popularity increased among his many friends whenever, on a long hike across the hills, he would suddenly start foraging in the ground to produce a couple of bottles of beer – planted there weeks earlier. There was no such sense of genius about Woods as there was with Ranji, for his achievements were gained by sweat and fierce determination. Both, though, were taken securely to the hearts of those who saw them and read about them in those faraway summers.

Braund, Hayward, Tyldesley

England's professional strength at the turn of the century rested with this kind of player: Len Braund (standing), a strong-nerved leg-spinning allrounder from Somerset via Surrey; Surrey's Tom Hayward (seated), a man who worked for his runs, made them in vast quantities, and expected to be paid properly for them; and J.T. Tyldesley, wearing the red rose of Lancashire and for a time the pre-eminent batsman from the North. Johnny Tyldesley excelled on difficult wickets, employing dapper back-play, cutting like a whiplash, and driving cleverly 'on the up'. Cardus wrote that 'an innings by Tyldesley, though moving on wings and enrapturing the senses, was always attending to the utilitarian job of building the Lancashire nest'. All three helped win Test matches against Australia, though Braund was sometimes punished on Australian pitches, his fabled accuracy wavering. Jessop once hit him for six boundaries in an over at Bristol. But Braund usually calmly came back with a wicket or two, a flashing slip catch, or a century when he batted.

LEN BRAUND, TOM HAYWARD, JOHNNY TYLDESLEY

WARNER'S TEAM TO USA, 1897

AMATEURS WITH CASH in their pockets and reserves in the bank could happily go off on jaunts to parts of the world where the click of ball on bat was less than deafening, and 'Plum' Warner, more than most, had a wanderlust and a passion for spreading cricket's gospel – while having fun – to go with it. With little warning, in September 1897 he got up a team to sail to North America for six matches, two of which were won, one lost, and three left unfinished. J.B. King shocked them in the match against Philadelphia at the Belmont Club, reducing them to four down without a run on the board, and finishing with nine for 25. It was the heyday of Philadelphian cricket. Much weaker sides have gone abroad under English flags. Standing are: G.L. Jessop, F.W. Stocks, A.D. Whatman, R.A. Bennett and J.R. Head. Seated are: W.M. Hemingway, J.N. Tonge, P.F. Warner, H.D.G. Leveson Gower and H.B. Chinnery. In front: F.G. Bull and H.H. Marriott. They managed to get their dazzling blazers through Customs without undue alarm.

C.L. TOWNSEND

THE SECOND OF FOUR generations of the family who played first-class cricket, Charlie Townsend was a schoolboy prodigy. Long-limbed and left-handed with the bat, he bowled right-arm leg-breaks which spun viciously, and was altogether too much for schoolboy opposition while playing for Clifton College. Gloucestershire blooded him when he was a mere sixteen, and in that first season of 1893 he established a unique record with a hat-trick of stumpings, W.H. Brain being the obliging wicketkeeper. In 1895, while still only eighteen, he claimed 131 wickets at only 13 apiece, though playing less than a complete season. In the home and away matches against Notts he took twenty-nine wickets, with fifteen against Yorkshire at Cheltenham, and a dozen each in the matches against Sussex, Surrey and Somerset. Even the most skilled batsmen were perplexed by his phenomenal spin. His batting developed, and in 1898 he did the double. By 1899 his batting had taken over: he amassed 2,440 runs at an average of 51, and did the double again. At last came Test honours, but his two appearances against Australia brought disappointment. It was to be another ten years before he showed the Australians what all the acclaim had been about by hitting an even-time 129 against them for Gloucestershire. By then he had put cricket into second place, having qualified as a solicitor. Young and brilliant, he had understandably been 'W.G.'s pet' – one of the more exciting meteors of the epoch.

The Gentlemen, 1899

A PICTURE OF AMATEUR might as the 1890s drew to a close. The Doctor, never one to appear insignificant in a group, wears his green-base London County blazer, blotting out the disagreeable memories of his departure from Gloucestershire. This was the year of his last Test appearance, and here he presides over his final match in the ranks of the Gentlemen at Lord's. He scored 78 before Mason ran him out, seeing his side to a total of 480. Fry (in front, centre) scored 104, but Mason, who scored 72, is missing from the picture, perhaps banished by W.G. for expecting too much of fifty-one-year-old legs. Between umpires Sherwin and West in the back row are Bill Bradley, who cracked open both innings of the Players, taking seven wickets for 154 in the match; A.C. MacLaren; and C.L. Townsend. Seated are Gregor MacGregor, the wicketkeeper; Ranjitsinhji, who made a charming 38; W.G.; and Major R.M. Poore, who learned to bat by reading, and returned to Hampshire with a vengeance this summer, scoring over 1,500 runs at an average of 91. In front are F.S. Jackson, C.B. Fry, and Digby Jephson of Surrey, who scattered the Players in disarray for 196 in their first innings by taking six for 21 with his underhand lobs. The Gentlemen won by an innings, but in the following year, 1900, it was the Players' turn to win at Lord's: they scored 502 for eight to win by two wickets, an extra over having been bowled after the official time for ending play. Though not universally approved of, Sammy Woods's gesture was considered by many as a fine and handsome piece of sporting etiquette.

COLIN BLYTHE, 'DICK' LILLEY, GEORGE HIRST

BLYTHE, LILLEY, HIRST

SOUTH, MIDLANDS AND NORTH blend into a yeoman combination, one which functioned in half a dozen Test matches. The one at Edgbaston in 1909 saw Hirst take nine wickets, Blythe the other eleven, while 'Dick' Lilley of Warwickshire enjoyed it all from his upright stance behind the stumps. There was something nearer amateur than professional about Lilley in his demeanour and lifestyle. Indulging in trap-shooting, he won a prize in Monte Carlo. He was thought of sufficiently highly to be invited to captain the Players, and was so much of an institution in the England Test team that he played thirty-five times – beyond even when he became a grandfather. George Hirst won only twenty-four caps, and failed in Australia, yet his name hovers higher than most of his protracted era, chiefly through his astonishing achievement in 1906 – over two thousand runs and two hundred wickets, quite magnificent, quite unique. Squarely-built and 'Yorkshire' in a quietly impressive way, Hirst had a heart which was large in competition – particularly when he was swerving the ball briskly into the batsman's tender groin – and glowing with warmth when it came to coaching the young, as he did at Eton of all places. Fourteen times he did the 'double', and his score of 341 at Leicester in 1905 remains a Yorkshire record to this day. He played regular first-class cricket until he was fifty – an age Blythe was destined never to see.

CHARLIE MACARTNEY

THE GOVERNOR-GENERAL they called him. But Macartney was more the dynamic subaltern, charging into the battle to sort out a threatening situation and, a couple of hours later, to have the enemy on their knees. He was small but wide, and he wore the cap-brim down towards his hawk nose. He liked to belt the ball back at the fast bowler's forehead. 'They don't like it, you know.' His confidence oozed out like the smoke from a smouldering fuse. 'I feel sorry for the poor coves who've got to bowl at me today,' he'd growl. And his team-mates knew it was no mere rhetoric. He had astonishing self-belief; and with good reason, for he had more than a little touch of genius. Earlier a slow left-arm bowler good enough to take eleven wickets in a Test against England in 1909, he rose to great heights in the 1920s, crashing 345 runs off the Notts attack inside a day and taking three successive centuries off England in the 1926 Tests, when he was forty. It all points to a cocky extrovert: but in fact he was a sensitive soul, often withdrawn, a virtual teetotaller, and said to be in tears as he sat in solitude in Sydney in later years watching inept and artless Australian batting.

YORKSHIRE, 1894

THAT YORKSHIRE SHOULD ever finish bottom of the County Championship, as they eventually did in 1983, was as unthinkable during the decades of unmatched glory as garish advertising hoardings around the boundary or the advent of international cricketers playing in pink and yellow trousers. The gathering strength of the white rose county was evident from the Championship success of 1893 – though Lord Hawke disapproved of the concept of a 'champion county' – and from the runners-up position in 1894, when this group sat. Almost completely professional, and disciplined under Hawke as never before, they won twelve of their sixteen county matches in 1894, instilling a pride throughout Yorkshire which was to last, with few troughs, well beyond the Second World War. The three players standing are Tom Wardall, Lees Whitehead and Joe Mounsey. Seated are 'Long John' Tunnicliffe, Bobby Peel, Lord Hawke, F.S. Jackson and Ted Wainwright. In front are J.T. Brown (of Driffield), David Hunter, the able and long-serving wicketkeeper, and George Hirst. The disunity of their county in the 1980s must surely have them rumbling in their graves.

J. T. HEARNE

THE TOP-CLASS PROFESSIONAL county cricketer was the man who gave his club value for money in terms of the right return of runs and wickets, week in week out; to whom his captain turned for the truth of the tactical situation at any time; who blended properly with the more glamorous amateurs; who was grateful for the privilege of a working life on sunlit turf; and who carved the Sunday roast in the pros' hotel. Jack Hearne was all of this. Modest and reliable, one of a famous clan of Hearnes, he bowled fast-medium and accurately for Middlesex and as an MCC professional from 1888 until after the First World War, trapping over three thousand batsmen,

and eight times taking nine wickets in an innings. In three summers he took over two hundred wickets, reaching 257 in 1896, the year in which he stunned the Australians by taking four for 4 and nine for 73 for MCC at Lord's. Three years later he performed the finest hat-trick of all time by dismissing Clem Hill, Syd Gregory and Monty Noble in the Test match at Headingley. Such was the respect felt for him that in 1920 he became the first professional to be elected to the MCC committee. He sits, before the hydrangeas, in the colours of Melbourne Cricket Club, who underwrote A. E. Stoddart's tour of 1897–98.

R. H. SPOONER

EGGIE SPOONER, one of the luminaries of the period, was invited to play for Lancashire when only eighteen, a product of Marlborough College. Instantly his bewitching style caught the eye as he scored 83 at Lord's against the demanding mixture flung down by Albert Trott. Soon Spooner was off to the Boer War, but upon resumption he continued to build a reputation which ranked with the best. The recommended time to watch Lancashire was before lunch, when MacLaren and Spooner opened the innings. Spooner was no stranger to centuries before lunch; nor to double-centuries, for he treated five areas of England thus: Old Trafford, Trent Bridge, Bath, The Oval and Leyton. And at Liverpool in 1903 he and MacLaren raised a record 368 for the first wicket off the numbed Gloucestershire bowlers. Spooner played in ten Tests, scoring a century against South Africa at Lord's in 1912, and won a rugby cap as well. His driving through the off side impressed itself forever into the minds of those who witnessed its wristiness. And yet, had he and his contemporaries been faced with the same torrent of short-pitched fast bowling from the start of the day's play until its end, as seen in 1984, the rich strokeplay would have been impossible, and there would have been no Golden Age.

THE LIGHTS WENT OUT. The rainbow blazers were discarded. On went the khaki uniforms. The bulbous black clouds which hung threateningly over the summer of 1914 had caused a sickening foreboding. When the storm broke over Europe, The Oval was commandeered for military use, forcing Jack Hobbs's benefit match to be switched to Lord's. Surrey cancelled their last two matches, so awesomely distracting had the war become. Although they still needed a few more points to secure the County Championship, no other county challenged Surrey's position. It was their first taste of supremacy since 1899.

Soon W.G. Grace was writing to *The Sportsman* urging that first-class cricket should stop immediately and that all players should join up to serve their country. 'There are so many who are young and able, and are still,' he wrote probingly, 'hanging back.' A year later he was dead, not long after having shaken his great fist at a Zeppelin as it floated high above his South London garden. When comparisons were suggested between the bombs tossed from the cockpit by German pilots and the bouncers that Australia's Ernie Jones used to fling down, the Grand Old Man observed that at least you could see 'Jonah's' lifters coming.

So very many of those whose names appeared in the county scoresheets of that final pre-war summer were soon to appear on casualty lists. So too were the names of youths who left public school playing-fields to don officers' uniforms, and working lads who were batting and bowling on club grounds and in parks one week and squelching through French and Belgian mud streaked with gore the next. The carnage was on a scale too stupendous for us truly to comprehend.

It had to end, the Golden Age. That it was shut off by such stark horror, bliss turned to grief, provided a contrast that intensified the dramatic impact. The colours returned eventually, though muted because the gaiety of life generally was less uninhibited, less ingenuous. World-weariness weighed down the spirit. While grace, gentility and good humour were never going to be banished from the English pattern of life, those commodities took on a cynical edge that was to become even more marked in the days of rabid materialism following the Second World War.

One beam of optimism spanned the Kaiser's war. It came from Lord Hawke's speech at the dinner in 1914 to mark the centenary of Thomas Lord's famous ground in St John's Wood. His Lordship could not prophesy what kind of place England would be one hundred years from that night, but he and his audience were convinced that Lord's and MCC would continue to flourish. Seventy years along the way, his faith seems to be justified.